ine

# Never Alone

By Frank Gregory

Unless otherwise indicated, all **Scriptures are taken from the** *Holy Bible, New Living Translation*, copyright © 1996. **Used by permission of Tyndale House Publishers, Inc., Wheaton, Illinois 60189. All rights reserved.**

Scripture quotations from the Holy Bible, New International Version®. (NIV®) Copyright © 1973, 1978, 1984 by International Bible Society. Used by permission of Zondervan Publishing House. All rights reserved. Scriptures marked (KJV) are taken from the King James Version of the Bible.

*Never Alone*
ISBN: 978-0-88144-507-7
Copyright © 2010 by Frank Gregory

Interior design and layout by Velin Saramov

Published by
Yorkshire Publishing Group
9731 East 54th Street
Tulsa, OK 74146
www.yorkshirepublishing.com

Printed in the United States of America. All rights reserved under International Copyright Law.
Cover and/ or contents may not be reproduced in any manner with out the express written consent of the author.

# Table of Contents

**My Story**

Chapter 1: Day of Deliverance ............................................. 11

Chapter 2: The Weight of Daddy's Boots ................... 19

Chapter 3: Moving Day ............................................................ 23

**God's Story**

Chapter 4: One Dysfunctional Family ........................ 27

Chapter 5: From a Cave to a Crown ........................... 33

Chapter 6: Pushed Out onto the Nile ......................... 39

Chapter 7: Surrounded by Hungry Lions ................. 43

Chapter 8: From Redeemed to Redeemer ................. 47

Chapter 9: Beauty at It's Rarest ..................................... 51

**Your Story (?)**

Chapter 10: A Place to Belong ....................................... 57

Chapter 11: The Mule That Would Not Die ............ 61

Chapter 12: Where Are You? ........................................... 63

Chapter 13: The Road to Healing .................................. 67

# Dedication

To Becky, my beautiful wife of twenty-seven years. Thanks for taking the pain of loneliness away.

# Acknowledgment

Thanks to Marilyn for all her hard work on helping to prepare the manuscript.

# My Story

# Day of Deliverance

I sat seething in my spirit. How could God do such a thing to me? Why had He tricked me? Was this what Jeremiah the prophet was meaning when he talked about "divine deception"?

It was January 1999, and I was attending a Pastor's Prayer Summit sponsored by International Renewal Ministries at Pine Cove near Tyler, Texas. I had been in my current pastorate for only about four months and had learned about the prayer summit through a mailer. It had caught my eye for several reasons.

First, I was both challenged and intrigued by the invitation to do nothing but pray for three days. These summits normally run from Monday through Thursday and are quite intense. I had never been to a meeting of this length with an agendum that was nothing but prayer. There are no speakers, no "how to" seminars, no featured singers, and no book signings. It is simply a time to get alone with God.

The second reason was an opportunity to get to meet other pastors in the Dallas/Fort Worth area. I have always been a networker and enjoy getting to know the other men I share the call to arms with.

The final reason was I needed this time. We had just experienced an extremely trying time the previous three years and had hit choppy waters almost immediately after our arrival in Texas. There had definitely not been a honeymoon period in this ministry. I had already been stretched, and it was not going to get any easier in the near future.

But I had come to pray and seek the face of God; not to share anything about myself, and that is why I was fit to be tied. During the morning of the summit's second day, Dick Palmer, the facilitator, told us that after lunch there would be a chair placed in the middle of the circle we had been sitting in and praying in. Each person in attendance would be welcome to sit in "the chair" and share any burden he desired to and be prayed over by the ones who felt compelled to come and pray over their brother. This is why I felt duped by God. I needed to be in that chair. There was a lot I needed to unload, but I did not want to do it.

You see, I grew up the only boy among four sisters. My dad died when I was nine, and I felt I always had to be the "man of the house" and stay strong. I did not do a lot of crying, and even after I was saved, I could still be pretty hard-hearted. I had been a three-year, three-sport letterman (I attended a small school) in football, basketball, and baseball; so to say I had been competitive is a total understatement. I did not have any use for wimps or the faint of heart. I certainly detested those people who could turn the tears on and off like a water faucet and guess what, I still do! However, I was beginning to see the value, even though crying and brokenness had not been for me as a rule.

So here was the decision I was confronted with, I could sit in "the chair" and share my heart and the needs in my life and let the chips fall, or I could be mute and basically go home knowing the whole trip had been a failure. This is not recommended for mulling over during lunch. Deep down in my heart of hearts, I knew what I had to do.

The afternoon session began with different men sitting in the chair and sharing. Some of these men had some pretty heavy-duty stuff, some of which I would not want to experience. This was no time, though, to be playing the spiritual comparison game. Neither was this the time to think I could vicariously do away with my need to share. It did not matter how many men I went up and prayed for, I still needed to share.

What I really needed to share with the men was the financial struggles we were experiencing at that time. We had experienced a significant loss in income at an already tough juncture in our lives just a couple of years earlier and we were still recovering. This was another area in which I had been ruthlessly hard on people in the past, and I felt a lot of shame for our struggles. I did not want everyone to see me for the way I was seeing myself—a big loser.

The pressure was getting intense by the time I started for the chair; it was almost as though I was out of body. I do not really remember walking to the chair. The next thing I knew, I was there.

I began to share the struggle we were having at that time. During the course of my sharing, I made reference to the fact of my father being dead and how difficult it was not having him to talk to during tough times. When I finished talking, the men began to gather around me to pray, and the meltdown began. I immediately began to weep almost uncontrollably and had gained a shaky handle on it when some men began to pray a different prayer. I thank the Holy Spirit for His ministry as He shows at times how we need to pray for people. Some of these men had been sensitive and picked up on the deep hurt in me that still remained after almost thirty years following my father's death. It was at that point they began to pray the abandonment away from me, asking that I could really know my heavenly Father in a very intimate way.

As these men began to pray in this specific way, it was as though the innermost emotions of grief began to erupt from my being. I had a liquidating sensation that can only be explained by the brokenness that God was allowing into my life. After this time of prayer had ended, I attempted again to semi-collect myself, not realizing the real crux of this time was yet to come. I am now going to have to pause in this story and go back a couple of months earlier.

Just prior to Thanksgiving of 1998, I had a dream that my dad was still alive. I had not had a dream like that in years, and it was so real. The dream took place present day. I was a grown man with my wife and children. In this dream, it was as though my dad had been gone for a long time and was back. I was so proud to show him to my three daughters and was delirious that he was still alive. As the dream ended, however, I was embracing him with a death grip and weeping beyond control.

I woke up that next morning both disoriented and angry. I was disoriented because my dad was still dead, and I was angry with God because He had even let me have the dream which gave me false hope. My mind was totally messed up that day. I tried to go to the office and concentrate on my work, but it was no use. I told my secretary when I went home for lunch that I would not be back.

I went home that afternoon and collapsed into bed like someone coming down from a high. When I woke up, I was still in somewhat of a stupor.

About two weeks later, my sister, Sammie, who lived near me, was relating a story to Becky and me. Our dad had died on her fifteenth birthday, and we were approaching both her birthday and his twenty-seventh death anniversary.

Sammie had gone into a boot shop to pick up some boots she was having repaired. When she was told the boots were ready, she began writing a check for the repairs. Just as she looked up from writing the check, she was eye level with a pair of boots that had the name Jack Gregory written on them. That was our dad's name! She was visibly shaken to the point that the shop attendant kept asking her if she was okay.

After Sammie finished telling the story, I began to question her about what day that had happened. We quickly came to the conclusion that she had seen those boots with our dad's name written on them the very same day I had my dream! We were just both looking at each other with huge question marks on our faces. Now fast backward to the prayer summit as I was standing; receiving hugs from some of the men, I felt more loved than I had in a long time. These were not just stiff "Lord-bless-you" hugs either. These were massive squeeze-the-life out-of-you bear hugs. When the men had finished hugging and affirming me, a man I had actually ridden down to the prayer summit with walked up to me. Though Gary was not an exact replica of my father, they had some similar features. My dad was tall and slender and so was Gary. My dad had dark hair he combed straight back and so did Gary. My dad had a kind, happy countenance and so did Gary.

Gary walked up to me and said, "For just a couple of minutes, I want permission to be your father." I agreed to this. Gary went on to say, "Son, I did not want to leave you, and it was not my choice, but I left you anyway. Now what I want you to do, son, is forgive me for leaving you because it was not something I wanted to do. Will you forgive me?"

Well, I lost it again. If you are counting, this is the third time I had turned to blubber. I was able to choke out an extremely shaky "Yes" to the forgiveness question. Gary then wrapped me up and said to me over and over and over, "Pappa God loves you."

This is where my dream had ended! Me hugging my dad and crying as if there was no tomorrow. What release God had brought to me in that moment! Needless to say, the remainder of that session was somewhat anticlimactic. I had unintentionally stolen the show.

I was in my room later that afternoon lying on the bed following a nap when my roommate, Bob, came in. He asked me, "Are you glad you did what you did today?" I sat there and said a quiet, confident "yes." There's more.

That evening when I went to dinner, I went early to have some time out on the dining hall deck to reflect. It was a crisp day with the sun setting behind me giving way to a clear blue sky. I looked up into that sky and said, "I love you, Daddy." I was finally telling my dad goodbye.

My dad had died on a Thursday morning, but I had last seen him on Tuesday night. He had already gone to work when I got up on Wednesday morning. Later that morning, he had an attack as the aneurysm was getting ready to rupture. He went into the hospital on Wednesday and died very unexpectedly on Thursday morning. I had never gotten to tell him goodbye and bring closure to his death. That day, when I told him I loved him, the journey toward healing began.

When I entered the dining hall, it was empty except for a woman who had come to the summit as an intercessor. These women had been meeting separately and praying for the pastors as we met together. When I sat down at a table, she approached me and asked if she could sit down and talk with me. I welcomed her company as she had already caught my eye as an anointed prayer warrior.

She introduced herself to me. Her name was Ann, and she has since become a surrogate spiritual mother to me.

When Ann saw my name, she related how the women had specially prayed for me that afternoon. She told me they had seen me as Timothy with a heart of purity that sought the favor of God; but the Lord had revealed to them in their praying that I needed a father! I said, "Have I got a story for you." Tears filled Ann's eyes as I narrated the events of that afternoon. The prayers of those godly women had been right on target.

What did God teach me from that time? I first needed to come to grips with the fact that my father, though unintentionally, had abandoned me. If you had walked up to me as a teenager and told me my dad had run out on me, I would have knocked you into next week. Deadbeat dads were the only ones who abandoned their families. God could not begin to heal me from the abandonment until I realized it was there. Abandonment had been the veil that had kept me from the intimacy I had longed to have with my heavenly Father. It had also given way to much anger in my life.

Second, no one does anything to deserve abandonment. Abandonment comes in all kinds of ways: death of a spouse, parent, child, sibling, close friend, etc., divorce, desertion, imprisonment and war to name some of the major causes. One of the weapons the enemy uses against victims of abandonment is to make them feel sub-human for being abandoned as if the pain of the abandonment is not enough already. You did not deserve to be abandoned.

Last of all, it broke the heart of God when my dad died and I was left without an earthly father. Please do not be angry with God and blame Him for your abandonment. I beg you to take the same hand you make the fist with and open it up to take God's hand and allow Him to pull you close to His heart.

Jesus experienced abandonment on the cross so we would not have to live with it forever. He seeks to bring healing to your wounded spirit. Will you run into His arms of love?

# The Weight of Daddy's Boots

"Franky, are you planning on going to school today?" This question was posed to me by my sister, Sue, as I was brushing my teeth. "Yeah" was my reply. "Do you really think you should go?" she implored further. "Why not?" I asked. "Because kids might be asking you questions like how Daddy died," she answered. I quickly decided I would not be going to school.

That conversation took place the day after my Dad had died. I was trying to get up and start my day with a "business as usual" attitude. As soon as my sister reminded me that kids at my school might want to discuss my father's death, reality once again set in like a truckload of bricks.

I don't know if I was thinking that going to school like a normal day would be the best therapy or if I was just trying to be the "man of the house" at the age of nine. Either way, I was in a survival mode without even realizing it.

I do not remember much else about the day in between. I am calling it that because it was the day sandwiched in between the day my Dad had died and the day of the funeral.

I do know it was a Friday, and it was still rainy and overcast. There was one event though, taking place that day that will have a lasting impression on me for life. It was an event that I had seemingly suppressed until last spring when I was sharing it over lunch with a man who has come to be a father figure to me in recent years . . .

I was in our kitchen that afternoon with someone when Sue came into the room weeping uncontrollably. She had just come from the funeral home and had seen our father dead for the first time. He had been made ready for funeral home visitation. As Sue was describing how he looked, I was not sure I even wanted to hear about it. After she was finished with the funeral home story, she asked me if I would go out to the pigpen and (what else) feed the pigs.

Feeding the livestock is one of my favorite memories that I have with my father. He would come in from work and eat supper. Then he and I, the men of the house, would go feed the cattle. We would go to the barn, and Daddy would load the hay onto the truck. I was still too short in the britches to throw a bale of hay around.

After Dad had loaded the hay, he would let me use his pocketknife, be it ever so carefully, to cut the baling twine. He would then drive the truck out into the pasture where the cattle were, and I would jerk out the baling twine and kick the hay off the truck as the cattle walked behind the truck waiting for it to drop.

The reason I was being recruited by Sue to go feed the pigs was because I had taken every step my daddy had taken, and I knew exactly how much corn and shorts (this was pig feed, not what we wear to play basketball in!) the pigs ate. These two pigs could probably more accurately be called hogs by now as they had grown considerably since we had gotten them, but I will continue to refer to them as pigs.

To get ready to feed the pigs, I stopped off at the utility room and put on my daddy's rubber boots. I wanted to make sure my feet were protected from all that mud.

Sue continued to cry as she walked with me out to the hog pen. When we got there, I went in while she stood on the other side of the fence and watched. Once I got inside with the pigs and fed them, something significant happened.

My daddy's boots began to sink in the mud up to about my ankles. As I tried to walk out of the hog pen, my feet started coming out of my dad's boots because they were still much too big and heavy.

I will never forget standing in that moment in time thinking, "Lord, my daddy's dead, and I am just trying to wear his boots to feed the pigs because they still need feeding, and I can't even do that." I cannot describe to you how small and helpless I felt all that time, thinking I could never fill my daddy's boots.

In that moment, my daddy's boots felt like they weighed a ton. Somehow, by the grace of God, I struggled to get out of the hog pen with the boots on. I eventually grew up and wore a lot of my daddy's clothes, especially his blue jeans, which I proudly donned my senior year of high school. I was glad to be big enough to wear my dad's jeans and know that God had healed a lot of the hurt. I never did, though, wear those boots again. They always seemed to be just a little too heavy.

Even though my daddy's boots were too big, my hurt was not too big for God to heal. He eventually gave me my own pair of boots to enjoy life in.

# Moving Day

"Wake up, Franky. It's time to get up. We're moving today." It was the voice of my sister, Sue. All I can remember thinking is, "No one asked me about moving." Although times have changed, I still do not think that three year olds are usually consulted about a family move.

Our family was about to move from our small twenty-acre farm in a small community called Nogo (that's right, No-go, like "no dough, no go," and save the jokes, I've heard them) twenty miles south to Hector—a much bigger community than Nogo, but still very small. Up until this time, I had lived in the same house and was very comfortable with it. The move was not going to set well with me. About all I can recall concerning the actual move was being quite upset that people were running over our picket fence. It had been laid down so that pick-ups could get close enough to our porch to load. I did not like that one bit, but knew my protests would have gone unheeded.

I can remember that night sitting on my mother's lap and crying while telling her, "I want to go home." The house we had just moved into was much bigger, but I was not impressed. The only thing I knew was that it was big and scary.

For three years my family lived there, I never did like that house and was very glad the day we moved out of it. It was not home, ever. This house gave me the first battle I ever had with the emotion of displacement. Displacement is something we all struggle with at certain junctures in our lives. Let me also point out that there is a distinct difference in *misplacement* and *displacement*.

**Misplacement** occurs when something is somewhere besides its proper place. It is not where it is supposed to be, but it does have a place it belongs.

**Displacement** occurs when you do not belong anywhere. You have nowhere to go. You are a fish out of water flopping for your life.

Believe it or not, God wants us to always have a measure of displacement. He never wants us to feel totally at home while here on earth. He does not want this world to become our comfort zone. For the child of God, heaven is our ultimate resting place where there are no misfits.

Remember the story of "Rudolph, the Red-Nosed Reindeer?" There is one part of the story where Rudolph and an elf named Hermie are on the Island of Misfits. Rudolph was there because of his nose, and Hermie was there because he wanted to be a dentist instead of doing the elf thing and making toys. But even when they get to the Island of Misfits, they find out they do not fit in. They are told that they are misfits among misfits.

Jesus died to make misfits *fit* in and winners out of losers. In the next several chapters, we are going to look at some people of the Bible who were misfits. They were all away from their homes and families for at least a generation, but God used each one of them in their abandonment to change world history. May their stories remind us all that God loves us no matter where we are and has a purpose for our lives.

# God's Story

# One Dysfunctional Family

I read about a family the other day that was in quite a mess. They would be prime candidates for family counseling in any cultural setting.

For starters, the father had multiple wives, and even other women who were his wives' servants had given birth to several of his children. Oh, and by the way, the two wives happened to be sisters.

One of the daughters had been raped and that led some of her brothers to wipe out all the men of the clan that the rapist was from. The brothers who did the killing did not play fair either, as the men they killed were fairly defenseless due to some strategic surgery the killers had performed on them just a few days earlier.

One of the men in the family unknowingly slept with his recently widowed daughter-in-law who was posing as a prostitute; and then of course he tried to deny it! The result of that single fling was twins.

There were twelve sons in this family, and any time you have that many boys, an entire football team plus the place kicker, you are asking for sibling rivalry. This family was no exception. Most of the intense jealousy, though, was directed toward one son! His ten older brothers hated this "daddy's boy" with a passion. So much that they wanted to kill him.

Now, brother-killing was nothing new—it's been around since, well, the beginning. Cain was so busy being jealous of his brother, Abel, that he forgot about pleasing God and killed Abel. Isn't that interesting? Of the first two children born into the world, one kills the other. It did not take long for the fall to make its full impact.

I once heard comedian Bill Cosby say, "If Cain did not like Abel, why didn't he move to Hawaii? He didn't have to kill him." Makes sense?

These ten brothers, though, did not end up killing their hated brother. They just sold him as a slave into a foreign country instead. To cover their tracks, they took his clothes and covered them with animal blood and told their father his son had been killed by a wild animal. How convenient.

I am sure most of you by now realize that I'm talking about the first family of Israel, Jacob's family. You want to talk about God's amazing grace; this family could have used it all up before Moses was even born! You may wonder how God could bring the Messiah from such a messed up family, but He did, and used this hated son to do it. He ended up saving their lives.

I often wondered what Joseph must have been thinking as he was led away to Egypt to be placed on an auction block. Here was the most favored son of the most favored man in the world being led around like a young bull at the livestock show.

What were you doing at seventeen? You were most likely getting ready to graduate high school and get on with the rest of your life, whatever that may have been. I can guarantee you that you were not being sold as a slave to the head of the Secret Service in a foreign land.

Every time I read this story, I have trouble trying to fathom that this could happen. I have come to realize in life that if you can't count on family; then whom can you count on? I don't think Joseph felt this way. His own blood had sold him out.

I have always lived believing that if the whole world turned against me, my family would still love and protect me. I am sitting here reading this story thinking if Joseph is in a foreign country as a complete stranger without any family, then who in the world is going to take care of him? His name is Jehovah, and he did quite well, thank you.

Joseph experienced abandonment like few people ever had. He was cut off from his family for more than twenty years, yet God used his abandonment to reshape world history. There is a spiritual principle at work here which ways, "The deeper the canyons, the higher the mountains." Let's get real. Most of us would love to have the position that Joseph eventually held, but how many of us are willing to go to prison while being wrongfully accused in the process? It takes a ton of trials to produce a few ounces of character.

The first life lesson I think God wants us to learn from this story is that He uses abandoned people, usually in a very powerful way. Our lives change quickly, without warning, and we must have the attitude that Joseph did, believing that a sovereign God is in control.

Another compelling truth that made an imprint on me from this narrative is that Joseph never forgot God. That also meant that Joseph never believed God forgot about Him. Every time Joseph is faced with a situation, he makes reference to God. How easy would it have been for Joseph just to blow off God and live life with the attitude that God, as well as everyone else, has forgotten about me, so I will just get everything I can and look out for number one? It is very easy for many people.

The first evidence we have that Joseph had not forgotten God is when Potiphar's wife attempts to seduce him. Here is a handsome, well-built young man in the prime of life with a chance to sleep with the boss' wife when no one is looking, and he responds like about a handful of young men in any time or culture would respond. He said, "No! And if you notice, he did not say no because he was afraid of losing his job, or of getting his boss' wife pregnant, or because he was afraid of getting AIDS or some other STD; he said no because of all things, it would be a sin against God. How did he come up with that one? I'll tell you how, even though Joseph was cut off from his father, he was not cut off from his teaching. He never forgot God even though it seemed to take him further down the spiral staircase.

When Joseph was in prison and was confronted with interpreting the dreams of his cellmates, he quickly acknowledged that all interpretations belong to God as he did when he stood before Pharaoh. That really took some guts, and God honored him in ways Joseph had never dreamed.

When abandoned, Joseph had a choice to make. He could forget God and become extremely bitter, or he could stay focused on God and let this thing play out to see what God was up to. Boy, oh boy, did he see.

When Joseph became vice president of Egypt and everything was great with his wife and 2.2 kids, you would think the story would end, and they would all live happily ever after. Not so, Jethro. God is bigger than that, and He is better than that. Even though Joseph was powerful and popular, he had a wound on his heart bigger than Texas (I am writing this chapter in Texas, so I know). Joseph had never forgiven his brothers. We all must forgive those who have abandoned us. It hurts and it's hard, but we must do it. If it were easy, we would not need God to help us.

One day, out of nowhere, actually Canaan, come ten brothers wanting to buy food because the famine has wiped out this wealthy family. Joseph goes out to see these ten brothers and discovers they were his. Was it tough for Joseph to forgive his brothers? About as tough as it would be for a Grand Canyon pack mule to win the Kentucky Derby. Without divine intervention, it's not going to happen.

So, after struggling with himself and locking up Simeon to let him know how it feels, and to let the other nine brothers sweat; and after making them think he is going to keep Benjamin for himself as a slave and make them go home and face their father, Jacob without him, Joseph chooses to make himself known to his brothers and to forgive them. You know what the interesting part is? Joseph wept louder than anyone did, which gives a slight indication of the release we feel when we forgive.

In his forgiveness statement, Joseph once again recognizes the hand of God in sending him to Egypt as a slave. God's grace never ceases to boggle my frail mind. Joseph's brothers abandoned him because they hated him and their actions end up saving their lives and reuniting the entire family . . . this time to live happily ever after.

So what are you going to do when you find yourself abandoned? Are you going to grab onto Jesus like never before or choose to become so bitter that no one can stand to live with you? Joseph gave new meaning to the phrase, "Tough times don't last, tough people do." His wild ride lasted more than twenty years, and he not only survived but also excelled because he refused to forget God.

# From a Cave to a Crown

The young man looked out onto the field he had stood on many years ago. He had wished 1,000 times he had never gone out there and did what he did. From his vantage point, it was cold, damp and musty; but then most caves have that feel.

Because he had gone to that field, his life was in the chaos he "enjoyed." You would have thought he had done something wrong with the way his world had been turned upside down, but it was quite to the contrary. What he did on this field that day had made him a national hero – the Boy Wonder of Israel as some would have it. When did it all go haywire? How could he end up like this?

He missed his mother and father. He especially missed his best friend, Jonathan. He was so homesick he even missed his brothers. He was the runt, the youngest. He knew his family understood why he had left, but it still ached inside. He still felt guilty, as if he had run out on them. Though he was the youngest, as it is many times, he had become the leader.

That day, though, he remembered it as though it was yesterday. His heart pulsated, his hands sweated, and his voice trembled as he shouted to the glory of God what he was about to do.

That was it! He had always tried to do only what God wanted him to do; nothing more, nothing less. He was so naïve and innocent to think that everyone else in the kingdom was going to appreciate that. Was he ever wrong!

So that is how it was for David, the shepherd boy, the soldier in Saul's army gone A.W.O.L., the future king of Israel, or whatever it was he was supposed to be, or more exact, whomever he was supposed to be.

After he killed Goliath, his name became an instant household word in the region. He literally went from a zero to a hero overnight (sorry, I just couldn't resist). Everyone loved David until those women sang that victory song. As the people were celebrating victory over the Philistines with a parade, the women began to sing a song that made Saul's blood boil. This was the song:

*"Saul has killed his thousands and David his ten thousands!"*
1 Samuel 18:7

David never could figure out what the big stink was. He had, after all, killed Goliath; but he had never written that song. That song began a process in which David eventually had to run for his life from a king insane with jealousy and landed him in this cave called Adullam.

We have all been to Adullam more times than we have wanted to be, and we will visit there again. It never feels right, never smells nice, and never gives us this warm feeling of how loved we are. Adullam makes us feel like David, abandoned and alone and wondering why we ever decided to obey God. He was still looking out on that field and remembering the day . . .

God loved David a lot, though, and sent him four hundred men to keep him company. These guys were known as David's 3-D men – men who were in *debt*, men who were *discontented*, and men who were just *disgusted* with life in general. They kind of sound like who you might find down at the corner bar. If they were around today, they would have bumper stickers that say, "Life sucks, follow David."

These were just the men David needed to keep him company in his state of depression; and were the people God was going to use in his life to teach him how to be a king. David just knew he had taken a wrong turn somewhere on his way to the throne. Listen closely to this, God does not have detours, His way is perfect.

David was abandoned and cut off and would remain that way for a while. What would get him to the place God had for him?

The difference in David being able to handle the abandonment that would have wilted most other men is found in 1 Samuel 16. The significance was not that David had been *appointed* as much as that he had been *anointed*. This one verse tells it all:

*"So as David stood there among his brothers, Samuel took the olive oil he had brought and poured it on David's head. And the Spirit of the Lord came mightily upon him from that day on. Then Samuel returned to Ramah."* 1 Samuel 16:13

Many times we make the mistake of wanting to run to 1 Samuel 17 to tell David's story; but there never would have been a 1 Samuel 17 if there had not been a 1 Samuel 16, and I am not just talking about chronology. Without the anointing of the Holy Spirit, we are nothing, and this is what got David from the cave of Adullam to the throne of Israel. I want us to look at three of the things the anointing accomplished in David.

First, it enabled him to do things he could never have achieved on his own. Without the anointing David never would have thought about taking on Goliath, much less killing him. God allows us to get in over our heads so that we learn to trust Him and not ourselves.

The second thing the anointing did for David was it sustained him through the caves, the hunger, the raiding parties, and the hot pursuit of Saul to take his life. When you are experiencing a layover to the great things God has for you, all kinds of people are going to take shots at you. This was true of David but probably never made clearer than with the story of Nabal.

Nabal was a mean and dishonest man who happened to be rich. David and his men encamped close to his ranch, and they provided protection for Nabal from raiders. When Nabal sheared his sheep, which was a time of celebration, David sent one of his young men to request provisions from Nabal. Nabal's reply was as follows:

> *"Who is this fellow David?" Nabal sneered. "Who does this son of Jesse think he is? There are lots of servants these days that run away from their masters. Should I take my bread and water and the meat I've slaughtered for my shearers and give it to a band of outlaws who come from who knows where?"*
> 1 Samuel 25:10-11

Nabal was a real swell guy. So swell that God struck him dead about ten days later. By the way, when God says, "Don't touch my anointed." He means it.

There have been many people on the road to great things that were scorned and ridiculed by losers just like Nabal. The anointing, though, helps you to keep your focus.

The final thing the anointing does is it will help you to maintain your integrity through all the displacement in life. One of the greatest verses ever written about David is in Psalm 78:

> *David shepherded them with integrity of heart. With skillful hands he led them.* Psalm 78:72 (NIV)

People do not wear the Star of Abraham around their necks; they wear the Star of David. Jesus is not sitting on the throne of Solomon; he sits on the throne of David. What is the most quoted passage in the entire Bible? Psalm 23. This is the beautiful passage of a shepherd writing about the shepherd and saying; "Thou anointest my head with oil." (KJV) David knew the anointing he had from God superseded any anointing he ever placed on a sheep.

How will you handle the road of displacement? A crown awaits you just around the corner.

# Pushed Out
# Onto the Nile

The Middle Eastern sun beat down upon his leathery skin. The ground below him was dry and hard. He skidded a lot through the sand and gravel as he scaled the mountain. He was not sure he liked what he had become, but like most things in life, it had just kind of happened. In his previous life in Egypt, shepherds were the dregs of society. How had he gone from a prince in the Egyptian court to a lowly shepherd on the backside of nowhere? He had never felt as though he belonged anywhere. Abandoned as a baby in the Nile River, Moses was abandoned by his mother who did the only thing she felt she could do.

Infanticide was the order of the day. His race of people was in the middle of a population explosion. This can be good unless you are under the rule of a paranoid king who is afraid of being outnumbered.

Moses was carefully placed into a basket that had been waterproofed and floated out into a shallow part of the Nile. Imagine the desperation of this mother to feel her baby was safer floating on the Nile than he was in her house. His mother and his sister watched from a distance to see what would become of this Hebrew baby who was only three months old. They were hoping he would be discovered by a merciful Egyptian who would not allow him to be killed, and did they ever hit the jackpot. Who should come down to the water to bathe but Pharaoh's daughter herself? She heard the baby crying and immediately had compassion on him. We know that's how he got his name, Moses, meaning "I drew him out of the water."

It seemed to be the perfect storybook ending. Here was a baby with a death sentence on him, only to be found, raised, and protected by the very one who had given it – the King of Egypt! What more could anyone ask for? There was restlessness, though, in his spirit. Although he enjoyed all the comforts that royalty had to offer, there was that growing sense of not belonging. There was also growing in him a determined desire to see justice among his people. Every day that passed brought a stronger disdain for what he represented. It grieved his heart to see how his people were being mistreated. So overwhelming in him was the urgency to right the wrongs that he did what we should never do – he played God. He saw oppression and took justice in his own hands by taking a life. This changed everything. Before the look and the smell of the palace had fully escaped his body, he was wandering in the desert. Good practice for what was to come.

On his desert journey, he once again becomes the righter or wrongs, only this time in not such drastic fashion. Some young ladies were trying to water their flock and were being harassed by shepherds. Moses comes to their rescue and ends up getting a wife out of the deal. You can see his plight and abandonment in what he named his first son. Gershom meant "I have been a stranger in a foreign land." Once again Moses thinks his life is set, and he will live in the Midian desert as a shepherd. That is until one day there was a fire.

God approached Moses in a way he had never approached anyone else that we know of. I am sure Moses was thinking that he was just minding his own business and trying to do his job. God, though, had a different job in mind. It still involved shepherding, only this time it was people and not sheep. God moves and God moves his people to where He wants them to be. He had moved them from Canaan to Egypt over four hundred years earlier, and now he was ready to move them back. There is quite a difference, however, in seventy and several million!

## For Such a Time as This

I am writing this chapter in the middle of a three-day fast. All I have had the past forty-four hours is bottled water. If you have ever fasted during an extended period of time, you know how morbid your breath can become. I am staying at a retreat center, and I opened my toothbrush container this morning only to find it empty! In a state of panic, I squeezed some toothpaste on my finger to rub on my tongue and then rinsed my mouth with the last .5 ounces of Scope that I had. Earlier this afternoon my breath was again needing, let's say "refreshed," but I did not want the Crest on the finger again. Out of mouthwash and with no toothbrush, I was just about ready for an emotional breakdown when I remembered possibly having a pack of Big Red gum in my overnight bag. I totally began to empty my bag of hotel soap and shampoos, along with shaving stuff and a few odds and ends. As I got to the bottom, I saw the pack of Big Red. A little worn and flattened, looking from being placed in there weeks ago, it greatly excited me. I love to chew gum. My wife tells me I do not chew gum. She says I chomp it. So, with Becky nowhere in sight and in her honor, I chomped on two pieces of Big Red to my heart's delight. Never had gum tasted so good, and never had my breath needed it so badly.

We are all like that pack of gum. We get buried so deeply sometimes by life that we feel as though God will never pick us up. Moses was so far on the backside of nowhere he probably thought even God did not know where he was. God always knows, and He never forgets. God brought Moses from a life of abandonment and used him to deliver a people thought to be abandoned by God.

God has purposed "for such a time as this," in all of our lives. We must be ready to listen, obey, and make the necessary adjustments to His purpose and break the abandonment.

# Surrounded by Hungry Lions

The joints in his knees ached terribly. He could not stay on them as long as he once could; so his daily discipline had taken a different posture than it had years ago when he was younger. Prayer had been a part of his daily regimen for years. So much was it a part of his life, it had become what defined him. Not only was he to be known as the consummate prayer warrior of his day, his name would be synonymous with prayer in every generation of many cultures for the next 2,500 years.

Praying had never been easy, though it had become less difficult. The primary motivation for praying was home. Home... what would it even be like now? He had not been there for almost seventy years. He had seen so much since he had been taken from his homeland as a teenager. Conspiracy, lies, deceit, and his three closest friends stare death in the face. Only intervention from their God saved them.

Living in a pagan land had a lot to offer a young man with political clout, much of it not good. He had overcome many temptations while making huge adjustments as his adopted kingdom had been ruled by different kings and most recently had been overthrown by a different country. He had seen kings and kingdoms come and go, but he never lost his love for home. That is why he faced toward the direction of home every time he prayed, which was three times a day. He wondered what home would even be like now. He had been whisked away so quickly. Were any of his family members even still living? He was sure his parents must be dead by now. His love and longing for home was a driving force behind his praying.

Even though prayer had proven to become an arduous discipline, it had never been quite so dangerous. His life had never been threatened for praying like it was now, but it still did not stop him from doing what he did most and best – pray. You see, most of us armchair prayer warriors cannot even fathom the intense focus that he possessed; but even he was now praying at a new level because Daniel was facing death for praying.

Before we get so focused on the fact that Daniel prayed, let us not forget whom he was praying to – the God of Israel. Daniel was surrounded by idolatry, but he never forgot where his hope was placed and where his tremendous anointing came from. It came from Jehovah. When confronted with death for their actions, the wimpy ones will stop while trying to save face and appease evil. Daniel was not about to do that. He knew that his honor depended on God and that God alone would either extend his life on earth or let it begin in heaven with Him.

You see, Daniel knew that prayer did not bring him death, it brought him life. The very act of crucifying ourselves when we pray keeps us from being destroyed by others. Daniel's enemies who were controlled by jealousy had yet to realize that. Darius loved Daniel, but he had allowed his ego to cloud his judgment when signing the edict into law. It is obvious he knew of Daniel's prayer habits. Interesting, isn't it? People know who prays and who does not; even though the people who pray call very little attention to it themselves. Even Daniel's dilemma had an effect on Darius' prayer life as it forced him to fast till the next morning.

Those lions sure did stink! Daniel was wondering when they had last had a bath. I try to imagine what it was like in the lion's den. We have all seen the pictures and heard the stories. I do not know if Daniel petted and played with the lions. God never saw fit to let us know if Daniel used the biggest, meanest lion for a pillow and slept. I do, though, know a few things.

First of all, no one ate that night. Daniel was not given dinner because he was supposed to be dinner. The lions did not eat because God took away their appetites and closed their mouths. Darius did not eat because he was just plain worried.

Second, it was probably very uncomfortable. This was supposed to be a death chamber, and it was not loaded with Lazy Boys. If you have ever tried to sleep on a rock and dirt, you know it can be a little rough.

Last of all, Daniel was not bored. When an angel drops by to save your life, it can be an exciting night. I doubt that Daniel even slept, and I bet he got the next day off. Once again, Daniel's prayer life caused a king to proclaim the God of Daniel as the only true and living God. Prayer works.

As far as we know, Daniel never made it to Jerusalem. He died in a pagan land. But we also know that Daniel did make it home. He rose again to receive the inheritance set aside for him.

# From Redeemed to Redeemer

Sweat flowed down her face like a waterfall. Her back and legs ached terribly as she constantly was bending over to gather the wheat. The sun beat down, and all the dust from the gleaning made it difficult to breathe. She looked forward to the end of the day. In all of her exhaustion and heat, her mind wondered back to what brought her here. Just a few months earlier she had been a happily married young woman with all sorts of dreams and a long life to look forward to with her new husband. A sudden turn of events, however, had drastically changed her life's course.

In just a brief span of time, she had experienced some tremendous stress that would rack up maximum points on any doctor's list of Valium candidates. This included being widowed as well as watching her mother-in-law have the same experience; and then a major relocation to a place she had never lived before. If she was to live fifty more years, which was highly likely at this point, she would never make sense of it all. Simultaneous to all of these rampant thoughts, a man stood at a distance watching her every move, finding her extremely attractive to the point he asked, "Who is that woman?" His attraction to her was not in her physical beauty but rather in her mental tenacity and her work ethic. It's great to have a beautiful wife, and it's even better when she knows how to work. That was one of the first things my Uncle Cleveland commented on about Becky. I had taken Becky home for the first time to meet the family. This was about a month before we were engaged. My mom told me later that my Uncle Cleveland had commented to her that what impressed him most about Becky was that after lunch she just wasn't sitting around looking pretty, but she was up helping do the dishes! My uncle and I were very close and his endorsement meant a lot to me. He co-signed for my first car, and I helped preach his funeral several years back. Ladies, I hate to break this to some of you, but you were meant to do more than lie around and look pretty. You most likely cannot afford to do that, unless you happen to be Tyra Banks. Nowhere in the Bible does it say that Ruth was a beautiful woman, but it is certainly implied in several passages. What was most attractive in her, though, was her strength of character. She was a woman full of compassion and devotion.

This was exemplified in her relationship to her mother-in-law, Naomi, more than any other person if you can believe that. You have to keep in mind that Ruth did not even have to be around Naomi because she was technically her ex-mother-in-law. She showed her compassion by helping her to relocate and making sure she was provided for. She showed devotion to her by embracing her God. This Jehovah God of Israel was one Ruth was not extremely familiar with but longed to know more about. His hand was already present in her life in a huge way without her even realizing it. This God had a plan and purpose for her that she could never have possibly dreamed or orchestrated.

This love story between Ruth and Boaz is one for the ages. What could simply have been deemed as a marriage of convenience was one that impacted every generation on earth after it. This union was much more than one to just grace the social section of the local paper. It helped to change world history and was deposited right into the family tree of Jesus. We might also want to mention that just three generations down, one of the little rug rats killed a giant on his way to becoming the greatest king in the history of Israel. Not bad for a woman who was fed by gathering the leftovers of the harvest. God just seems to work like that.

    The biggest immediate winner in all of this was Naomi. She finally had the grandchild she so desperately wanted, and her family name was preserved. All of this happened because of Ruth's heart for God. She was a gift literally laid at the feet of Boaz. He was sensitive and caring and did not take advantage of the situation. Their story of love is one that will never die.

# Beauty at It's Rarest

Her eyes pierced your heart with an honesty that stopped you in your tracks. Her flowing hair surrounded a face that displayed wisdom and understanding. Her royal attire hung on her slender frame and spoke grace with every movement. She was a beauty queen. The first Miss Universe. She had competed against 126 other young women and won. She was more than a beauty queen, much more. You see, she was *the queen.*

From the most humble of beginnings, God had raised her up. She was an orphan raised by a relative, and with this seldom mixture of beauty and humility, she stole the hearts of a nation, especially the heart of the king. And it would take it all – everything she possessed from her resilient spirit to the calculated risks to save her people. That's what it would take for Queen Esther. The Persian Empire ruled the world and the Jews who had gone into captivity under the Babylonians were now in the regime of King Xerxes. The people of Persia had great respect for the law, and it could not be reversed by anyone once it was sealed with the signet ring of the king. Queen Esther was being closely watched by her cousin, who had also been her guardian. His name was Mordecai, and it was his immutable will that triggered the events of this time. There was an extremely pompous state official who loved to prance around the palace and have everyone bow to him. His name was Haman. What Haman probably did not realize, however, was most of the people that bowed were just out to win some brownie points. You see, "sucking up" was in vogue, even in biblical times.

Even though bowing to Haman was not required, it was strongly recommended. Mordecai had the moxie, though, not to do it. He just was not as impressed with Haman as everyone else seemed to be. This lack of respect and admiration shown by Mordecai incensed Haman to no end. He grew to develop a vehement hatred for Mordecai to the point that no other amount of adoration shown toward Haman even seemed to compensate. It was Mordecai who rained down thunderstorms on Haman's parade. This is where Haman made the fatal mistake of his life. He greatly overestimated his power and influence while grossly underestimating Mordecai's clout. Haman does not have a clue that he is about to agitate the queen's greatest influence.

Haman made the error we all have made from time to time. Anytime we allow the great killer known as pride to make our decisions, we are doomed before we even get started. Haman allowed his pride to make Mordecai and his destruction his total focus. We should never allow another human, for good or bad, to dominate our lives in such fashion. To carry out his dastardly plot of extermination, Haman must have the cooperation of the king, and this is where the plot began to thicken. Haman went to King Xerxes and asked him to issue a law calling for a slaughter of the entire Jewish race. The king acts on blind trust and signs the decree into law; sealed with his signet ring. Mordecai is devastated when he hears the news. He puts on clothes of mourning (dressed in black just like Johnny Cash) and refuses to eat. Esther hears of this and becomes concerned and sends messengers to inquire of his well-being. Mordecai's reply is not necessarily one Esther wants to hear, but her father figure tightened the vise. He basically tells her that her entire race is on the verge of extinction unless she mediates on their behalf. Esther is definitely knocked out of her comfort zone and wonders why all the pressure is being placed on her. Mordecai reminds her that she has been strategically placed for such a time as this. This is when Esther, the little orphan girl, becomes the hero.

She goes to the king, fully aware that she could be executed if he fails to extend the golden scepter. Esther puts her life on the line for the salvation of her people. It is a fair assumption that Esther still had not come to the realization of just how wrapped the king was around her finger. He was willing to give her anything she wanted up to half the kingdom. Keep in mind we are not talking about Rhode Island. Esther eventually pled her case to the king on behalf of her people, and even though the original law cannot be reversed, they were given consent to defend themselves. This beautiful, yet humble young woman had saved thousands of lives. Though she was far from home, God used her beyond anything she could have imagined. Joseph and Esther both preserved Israel, though at different times and in different ways, the mission was still accomplished. Oh, and by the way, Haman was hung on the gallows he had built for Mordecai.

Feel left out and abandoned? God could be preparing you for your finest hour!

# Your Story (?)

# A Place to Belong

Our lives are intertwined with others during our seasons of life. Rarely are there people that we go "wire-to-wire" with outside of family. No, most people are there for a time. Our lives are broken up into several segments. There are the people we went to school with, then the ones we knew in college. After that come the people we know from our jobs and even different places that we live. Some make a lasting impression while others we barely notice. Some leave us with good memories; some not so good. Either way, they all are a line in our story.

Such was the case of one of my best childhood friends – Bobby Lusk. I can remember the first time I ever saw Bobby. It was the spring of 1972, and I was with one of my sisters to pick up my sister Sammie from church. We had not attended that evening and were outside watching everyone come out. I can remember seeing a new family walk out and wondering who they were. We inquired of Sammie when she got into the car, and she said it was a new family from Texas. After that, we almost became immediately acquainted with Robert, Virginia, and Bobby Lusk. By that summer, they were some of our closest friends. I don't know all the reasons they came to Hector, Arkansas, but I know we were one of them. God sent them into our lives at a very strategic time.

My dad had died just a few months earlier, and they helped to greatly ease the pain. They lived in a small house that reminded me of the cozy cottages I had read about in books. I never felt more at home in another place than I did there. Robert and Virginia were not wealthy. They were just generous. You did not have to be a genealogy expert either to figure out Bobby was not their biological son. Bobby had been adopted by Robert and Virginia off an Indian reservation when he was only a year old. How blessed he was to have been chosen by this family! His dark skin even provoked some racial slurs when he first moved to our segregated community, but he soon fit in with the rest of us. Though he was a couple of grades behind me, we soon became inseparable at church and on weekends. One of my many good memories was of us asking Robert, who was a deacon in our church, if we could have a television installed in our little church building so we could see the end of the Dallas Cowboy games. Bobby and I stayed close until a couple of years after I graduated high school, and we probably have not seen each other more than ten times since then. We spoke often and openly, though, about his adoption, and it never seemed to be a problem.

Adoption is what this chapter will deal with. I do not know about it from a personal experience. All of my siblings and I are biological brothers and sisters. My three daughters were given birth to by my wife and fathered by me, whether they want to admit it or not. However, people who are adopted can really struggle with feelings of abandonment and displacement. Sometimes even emotions of betrayal can surface, especially if the one adopted has to find out by him or herself. I know it is not always easy to make the call when you are a spectator, but I would always advise letting the child know as soon as possible. Sometimes, as in Bobby's case, it is much more apparent with the glaring ethnic differences, while at other times, even the most intimate friends are unaware of the situation.

My perspective of adoption changed even more a few years ago during a church gathering where I had the director of the local crisis pregnancy center address our congregation. This ministry was also getting involved in the adoption side of unplanned pregnancies. When Angie asked us how many of us were adopted, very few, if any, hands went up. She then went on to explain that everyone who had come to Christ was adopted. You see, none of us are born into God's family by natural birth. We became part of God's family through faith, and Paul in several places literally uses the word "adopt," describing how we come into our heavenly father's family. That, my friend, is exciting. Adoption simply means becoming part of a family in which there is no biological connection. In fact, in biblical times, adopted children were often held in higher regard than natural born descendants. This was largely in part to the adopted child being "chosen" by his parents. Adopted children have literally changed the course of history and made an impact for the kingdom of Christ that only eternity will tell. You have heard it talked about that George Washington was known as the "Father of our Country" without ever fathering any children of his own. What most people do not realize, though, is that George Washington actually adopted a daughter.

One of my mentors, Leighton Ford, was adopted into a very godly family that helped make him into one of the greatest evangelical leaders of our time. Who knows what could have happened if he had not been adopted. The list of adopted children is in the millions, but just to name a few: Dave Thomas, founder of Wendy's, whose foundation still continues to change lives through adoption. Winston Churchill, who almost single-handedly saved Europe during World War II. Nancy Reagan, who was an extremely influential first lady, and as you may have guessed, was adopted. The list almost seems endless.

Let me tell you, I am a big believer in divine providence, and I believe God has used adoptions to rewrite world history.

Adoption is not a dirty word. If you happen to be adopted, let me give you some steps to take in the healing process. These apply whether you know or are yet to find out.

Number one, forgive yourself. It was not your fault that you were born. Stop blaming yourself for being adopted – something you had no choice in. Secondly, forgive those who gave you up for adoption. Whether you think the circumstances could be justified or not, it does not matter. Let it go and forgive them. By being bitter and resentful you are only hurting yourself. Next, you need to be thankful for the people who did adopt you. Let them know again how much you love them and appreciate what they did. Last of all, celebrate your adoption! Throw a party, call a friend, and buy a car (just kidding). But do something to let yourself know how blessed you are. Embrace your adoption with all the joy within you.

I want to close this chapter by reminding you that the person who continues to change the world more than anyone was adopted. I think it took a lot of guts for Joseph to step up and take Mary, who was carrying a child that did not belong to him, to be his wife and consent to raise this baby who came to be known as the Messiah.

Back to my friend, Bobby, I guarantee you if Bobby was asked if he regretted being adopted, his reply would be a resounding no. He would tell you that he could not have picked better parents if he was given ten years to decide. Adoption is definitely a way to go. I am glad God thought of it.

# The Mule That Would Not Die

She stood with her face pressed against the window and stared for so long that eventually there was nothing there. The young girl was seeing her father for the first and last time that day. That was over fifty years ago.

She was born to a single mother back in the early 1940s. This was not a real common occurrence in those days, especially in rural Arkansas. Her mother was one of thirteen children, so she was raised along with the younger siblings who were actually her aunts and uncles. Even though she was the oldest of the thirty-two grandchildren, the rest of us always referred to her as "aunt." Her story is sad. She was born to a mother in her early twenties who would never live to see her thirties. Her mother died at the age of twenty-nine from a rheumatic heart. Joan was only eight. She was raised after that by her grandparents. When she was about twelve years old, something so bizarre happened that I do not think it could have even been scripted in Hollywood; and the chain of these events literally brought her father right into her yard. Her paternal grandfather, who lived miles away, owned a mule that became lost during a storm. The mule became sick from eating wet grain and wandered up in my grandpa's yard where Joan was living and fell dead! My grandpa had to make contact with the mule's owner by radio through the Forest Service. Soon after that, the owner and his son (Joan's father) came to get the mule and drag it away. My mother, who was already married, happened to be at her parents' house that day. As Mom sat there holding my oldest sister, she could see Joan's dad out in the yard. She asked Joan, "Joan, do you want to see your daddy?" Joan answered yes, and my mother told her he was standing right outside in the yard. Joan made her way to the window and gazed out until no visible images remained. She never spoke a word to her father, even though her attempts to make contact years later turned out to be futile. In spite of this, Aunt Joan went on to have a happy life. She married a loving husband and gave birth to their only daughter, who gave her two grandsons.

She is one of my heroes. I never saw her be bitter or hateful, or use her circumstances as an excuse for anything. Instead of being a victim, she chose to be a victor! You may have a story quite similar to Joan's. What will you choose to be? The choice is truly yours, and no one else can make it for you. For your sake and everyone else's around you choose life.

**Post Script**
Not long after finishing this chapter, Aunt Joan died. I so regret she was not here to read it. When I join her in heaven, we will have plenty of time to sit down and visit about it.

# Where Are You?

Abandonment visits at seemingly the most inopportune times, and in different "packages," if you will. As we begin to put a close to this story, the intent of this book is not to leave you hanging, but rather to help you pinpoint at what level you have been affected and then find healing in your spirit. I am going to break up abandonment into four levels or stages. Let me say I am not an expert on this subject, nor am I a psychologist or licensed counselor. My heart in writing this book is to help people identify and deal with the level of abandonment they have experienced. There is nothing scientific about this, but perhaps it will give you a starting point in the healing process.

The first level of abandonment we will *call short-term abandonment*. This could be anything from a few hours up to several months. This is the most common form and affects the most people. This is the child who is left alone by his parents who is really not sure where they are and when they will return. These are the kids whose father or mother is on a substance abuse binge and is missing for several days. This could also include people who deal with a vacancy created by service in the military, imprisonment, or a vocation that lends itself to being gone for weeks at a time. This is the most subtle and least recognizable level because it is temporary but can still have long lasting effects.

Next is *long-term abandonment*. This can last anywhere from a few years to a lifetime. This can include such circumstances as divorce, desertion, adoption, being separated at birth or in early childhood from siblings, or an extended prison sentence. This is when the separation has been so long it is as though you are meeting someone for the first time. These are the kinds of scenarios that make for novels and talk show material. These reunions can be extremely joyful for the people involved. They can also be filled with questions and a lot of emotional scars.

The third level of abandonment is the toughest to live with in this life, and that is **final abandonment**. This is when we deal with a vacancy created by death. We will never have that person here with us on earth again. The best description I can give of how it feels is numbness. You just cannot believe what you are hearing. It is almost as if you are expecting to wake up from a dream and expect that person to be there. Once the numbness wears off, you have this overwhelming feeling of grief to the point you are being swallowed up by your emotions. This later can turn into tremendous anger. It is possible for this all to happen within hours of receiving the news. There is nothing in this life that is harsher to deal with than the death of a loved one. You are changed for life. You can feel cold on the most beautiful spring day. Your world as you knew it has ended.

The final level of abandonment is eternal. This is when a person dies without a relationship with Christ and is condemned to hell forever. I realize this is not a popular subject, and I am probably going to lose some readers here, but it does not change the truth. I believe in a literal burning hell where people without Christ will spend eternity. To me, though, the physical torture is no comparison to psychological insanity a person experiences. Jesus called it "outer darkness," and it involves being cut off from God and everything He has created forever. It is the worst form of solitary confinement you can imagine.

I have experienced the first three levels of abandonment, and you probably have also; but the good news is we do not have to experience the fourth. God does not want you to go to hell because He gave His son to die for us. Accept Jesus Christ as your Lord and Savior today. The first three levels cannot hold a light to the eternal one.

If you find yourself struggling at any of these levels (except the fourth one of course), there is hope for you. That's the great thing about life; as long as we are breathing, there is always hope. Hope is the most powerful thing we have.

# The Road to Healing

*We are pressed on every side by troubles, but we are not crushed and broken. We are perplexed, but we don't give up and quit. We are hunted down, but **God never abandons us**. We get knocked down, but we get up again and keep going.*
2 Corinthians 4:8-9

I do not pretend to know everything about this subject, not even close, and I hopefully have not given that impression throughout this writing. There are many experiences with abandonment I hope to never have, and there are many others I still have to experience unless I die first. What I hope to do now, though, is to help you get on the road to healing in your spirit. How I wish something like this would have been handed to me twenty years ago. We have hopefully helped identify where you are in your sojourn. Now maybe we can help you to shake the demons and get on with your life.

The first thing you need to do is deal with your anger. It is okay to be angry. You just do not want to reside on Anger Street the rest of your life. Step one is realizing and admitting to your anger.

Next in the process is who are you angry at? Is it a parent, a sibling, or some significant other? Are they dead or alive? Many people find themselves adamantly angry at God. Let's deal with God first because He has always been the human race's cosmic punching bag. You have no reason to be angry at God. It is not His fault. God's plan for everyone's life is joy and peace, but the reality is we live in a fallen world, and people hurt other people. People get sick and die, and lots of stuff happens all because of sin. God never intended for us to be here forever. He has a much better place in mind. Do not be afraid to tell God you are angry at Him. He is big enough to handle it. I have yet to hear of God being knocked off His throne.

One of my favorite scenes in the movie "The Apostle" is where Robert Duvall's character, "Sonny," is telling God, "I am mad at you." I think when we tell God those things He just smiles at us and says, "That's OK. I still love you more than you'll ever know." As I said in the beginning, God wants you to unclench that fist and take His hand. He desires to heal you and lift you out of your anger. God gets angry so He knows how you are feeling. I can guarantee you if you have been abused or victimized, God has been angry for you. If you are someone, however, who thinks God is sitting around waiting to shoot lightning bolts out of His fingers every time you mess up, get way over it! Realize that God is your Heavenly Father who has your best interests at heart. He is always there for you.

What if you are angry with someone who is already dead? That's a tough one. The best advice is let the person know. Have a one-way conversation. Write a letter and leave it on the grave. Have a person stand in for that individual so you can physically talk to him or her (remember, this is something I did in chapter one). What you must comprehend is the fact that you still need closure.

What about reconciling with someone still alive? Know that there are two kinds of reconciliations. The first is one-way reconciliation. This is where the person is unwilling to communicate with you in any way. As is often said, you cannot control that person, but you can control your reaction. Forgive the person and let him or her know you are available any time to talk. Remember, they are hurting worse than you. If the person is willing and available, then you must keep in mind that restoration is the ultimate goal. The best way to meet is in person. If that is not possible, then communicate by phone and last of all in writing (letter, e-mail, IM, etc.). This is not the time for attacking but rather for healing. Unforgiveness only makes you ugly and bitter. It has put many a person into an early grave. There is a great line in the movie "Wall Street" about a man looking into the abyss and finding his character. Let me tell you, I have been to the abyss. I have been so on the brink of wanting to end it all that I even had it planned. Never once, though, in my darkest of moments did I feel totally alone. I know God was patiently waiting for me just as my mother did when I would come home at night and go into her room and let her know I was home.

Your Father waits for you right now, wherever you are. All you have to do is call out to Him, and you will never have to feel alone again.